PROPERTY OF
WHITTIER SCHOOL
LIBRARY
NORTHLAKE, IL.

GRANDMA LOIS REMEMBERS

Text © 2002 by Ann Morris
Photographs and illustrations © 2002 by Peter Linenthal
Designed by Carolyn Eckert

Other photographs courtesy of Alabama Department of Archives
and History, Montgomery, Alabama: p. 14; Birmingham Public
Library Archives: pp. 15 (catalog # 8.08), 17 (catalog # 21.80), 21; the
Sanders family: pp. 18, 24, 25, 32

Library of Congress Cataloging-in-Publication Data

Morris, Ann, 1930–
Grandma Lois remembers : an African-American family story / Ann Morris ;
photographs and illustrations by Peter Linenthal.
p. cm. — (What was it like, Grandma?)
Summary: An African American grandmother relates family and cultural
history to her grandson in their Queens, New York, home as she tells of
growing up in segregated Birmingham, Alabama. Includes a recipe and
the words to Amazing Grace.
ISBN 0-7613-2316-3 (lib. bdg.) 0-7613-1729-5 (pbk.)
1. African American families—Alabama—Birmingham—Juvenile literature
2. African Americans—Alabama—Birmingham—Social life and customs—
20th century—Juvenile literature 3. African Americans—Alabama—
Birmingham—Social conditions—20th century—Juvenile literature 4.
African Americans—Alabama—Birmingham—Biography—Juvenile literature 5. Grandmothers—Alabama—Birmingham—Biography—Juvenile
literature 6. Birmingham (Ala.)—Social life and customs—20th century—
Juvenile literature. 7. Birmingham (Ala.)—Biography—Juvenile literature.
8. Birmingham (Ala.)—Race relations—Juvenile literature. [1. African
Americans—Alabama—Birmingham—History. 2. Birmingham (Ala.)—
History.] I. Linenthal, Peter, ill. II. Title.

F334.B69 N457 2002   976.1'78100496073—dc21   2001044084

The Millbrook Press, Inc.
2 Old New Milford Road
Brookfield, Connecticut 06804
www.millbrookpress.com

All rights reserved

Printed in Hong Kong
library edition 5 4 3 2 1
paperback   5 4 3 2 1

What Was It Like, Grandma?

GRANDMA LOIS REMEMBERS

An African-American Family Story

Ann Morris

Photographs and illustrations by Peter Linenthal

The Millbrook Press

Brookfield, Connecticut

Erick watches his sister, Nakia, play the piano while the whole family sings.

Erick is one of those lucky children who comes from a large family.

He lives in a house in Queens, New York, with his mother, father, older sister, Nakia, and older brother, Phenize. His Grandma Lois lives in a house nearby with her husband, James, but she often stays over. Often Erick's uncles, aunts, and cousins stop by to visit.

Erick's mother, Naomi, works as a librarian in a nearby school. Sometimes she reads stories to the children who visit the library where she works. Erick's father, Erick Sr., works for the government. Erick's sister and brother go to college, but they come home on holidays.

Erick's mother was the first person in the family to go to college. The family is very proud of her. Erick is eight years old, but he is already thinking about going to college, too. He wants to be a brain surgeon.

Erick's school is not far from his home. After school Erick has fun kicking around a soccer ball outside his house.

Erick has a special relationship with each person in the family.

His mother and father, of course, care for him very much and see that he has everything he needs.

Phenize plays ball with him and cheers him up when he is feeling sad.

Erick and Phenize

Nakia takes him to the playground. They are pals. Sometimes Erick pushes Nakia on the swing.

When the rest of the family is away, Grandma Lois often stays home with him.

Erick and Nakia

Grandma Lois is a quiet, thoughtful woman.

She is devoted to her church and has been an usher there. She also served as president of its governing board.

Grandma Lois spends many hours reading the Bible. Sometimes she reads it aloud to the whole family. She also enjoys books on religion and African history.

Erick loves books, too. In fact, the whole family likes to read.

Grandma Lois enjoys telling family stories to her grandchildren and sharing her old family album.

As the family looks at the photographs together, Lois tells the children what life was like when she was little.

Downtown Birmingham long ago

Grandma Lois was brought up in Birmingham, a big city in Alabama.

Downtown Birmingham had many large buildings, shops, hotels, and restaurants.

Grandma Lois remembers riding the trolley that ran through the city. It was fun. But, she also remembers that African Americans had to ride in the back of the trolley.

Blacks and whites lived separately in Birmingham then. Blacks were not welcome in white schools or white neighborhoods. They were not allowed to mix with whites in restaurants or on buses, trains, and trolleys. Grandma Lois said that black and white people had to use separate drinking fountains.

An old trolley car

Lois's father worked in one of the many steel mills in Birmingham.

He was lucky to have such a good job because at the time it was hard for African Americans to get good jobs there.

Birmingham steel factory

Grandma Lois (right), about four years old,
with her brother, Lawrence (left), age three

Grandma Lois says that times were tough when she was growing up, but her family was better off than many African-American families. They had a house with a big porch at the edge of town in an African-American neighborhood. They had a car, a wind-up record player, and they were one of the first families in their neighborhood to have a radio. When Lois was little, they did not have running water or electricity in their house.

Lois remembers walking to school. Her favorite subject was math. She remembers learning to cook and to tell stories.

And she remembers the fun she had playing with her little brother, Lawrence, and her many cousins.

Sundays were very special when Lois was growing up.

In the morning the whole family would go to Sunday school and then to church. After church they would have a big Sunday dinner of fried chicken, sweet potatoes, collard greens, corn, and sweet potato pie. Lois's six aunts usually came for Sunday dinner. Sometimes their pastor would join them. Because there were so many people at the table, the adults would eat first and then the children.

In the evening the family would go back to church for evening worship.

Grandma Lois went to this church when she was a girl.

"What kind of games did you play when you were little?" Erick asks Grandma Lois.

She tells him that she liked to jump rope and to play hopscotch, marbles, and checkers.

Lois still plays checkers today. She and Erick are checkers partners.

He learns special moves from her.

Grandma Lois moved to New York when she was twenty-one years old.

When she was twenty-eight, she married Erick's grandfather, James. The couple soon had five children.

James worked as an orderly in a hospital. Lois worked at home caring for the children. Later, when her children had children, she helped care for them, too.

Lois and James as a young couple

Grandma Lois caring for Nakia, Phenize, and another grandson, Fred

Throughout her life, Grandma Lois has loved music.

She and Erick play the piano together.

Sometimes as they play the whole family sings the many hymns that Grandma Lois has taught them. Their favorite is "Amazing Grace."

Amazing Grace

A-maz-ing grace! How sweet the sound

If you know the tune, you can sing
"Amazing Grace," too. Here are the words:

Amazing grace! How sweet the sound
That saved a wretch like me!
I once was lost, but now am found;
Was blind, but now I see.

'Twas grace that taught my heart to fear,
And grace my fears relieved,
How precious did that grace appear
The hour I first believed.

Through many dangers, toils and snares,
I have already come;
'Tis grace hath brought me safe thus far,
And grace will lead me home.

The Lord has promised good to me,
His Word my hope secures;
He will be my shield and portion be,
As long as life endures.

Yea, when this flesh and heart shall fail,
And mortal life shall cease,
I shall possess, within the veil,
A life of joy and peace.

The world shall soon to ruin go,
The sun refuse to shine;
But God, who called me here below,
Shall be forever mine.

When we've been there ten thousand years,
Bright shining as the sun,
We've no less days to sing God's praise
Than when we'd first begun.

Sweet Potato Pie

Makes eight servings

SAFETY TIP:

If you try this recipe, get an adult to help.

HERE IS WHAT YOU NEED:

3	eggs
1	cup sugar
1/4	cup melted butter
1/3	cup milk
1	teaspoon cinnamon
1	teaspoon nutmeg
1 1/2	cups cooked mashed sweet potatoes
2	tablespoons lemon juice
1	teaspoon vanilla
1	large unbaked pie shell (in a baking pan)

HERE IS WHAT YOU DO:

1. Preheat the oven to 350° F.

2. Put the eggs and sugar in a bowl and beat together.

3. Add the butter, milk, and spices. Mix well.

4. Add the mixture to the sweet potatoes in a large bowl.

5. Add the lemon juice and vanilla. Mix well.

6. Pour the mixture into the unbaked pie shell.

7. Bake for 50 minutes, or until the pie is brown.

8. Let the pie cool. Serve.

Grandma Lois used to help her mother in the kitchen.

She learned to cook some family favorites—fried fish and chicken and sweet potato pie. She would go to the farms near her home in Birmingham to get the sweet potatoes.

These days the whole family helps Grandma Lois make her special sweet potato pie, especially when everyone gathers together on holidays.

Erick's whole family really loves sweet potato pie.

And of course they all enjoy eating their share!

ALL ABOUT MY FAMILY

Would you like to know about your family? Here are some things you can do.

INTERVIEWS

You will find out many interesting things about your relatives by interviewing them. Ask them questions about their childhood—where they lived, what they liked best to do and to eat, what they read and studied in school. Find out, too, how things are different today from when they were young. Use a tape recorder to record your questions and their answers.

FAMILY ALBUM

Ask your relatives for pictures of themselves. Put all the pictures in an album. Write something you have learned about each person under his or her picture.

FAMILY TREE

All of us have many relatives. Some of us are born into the family. Others are related by marriage or have been adopted. You can make a family tree that looks like the one on the next page to show who belongs to your family.